HERE WE GO

AND

ESCAPED ALONE

T0151859

OTHER PLAYS BY CARYL CHURCHILL
PUBLISHED BY TCG

HERE WE GO
AND
ESCAPED ALONE

Two Plays by

Caryl Churchill

THEATRE COMMUNICATIONS GROUP
NEW YORK
2016

Here We Go is copyright © 2015 Caryl Churchill Limited

Escaped Alone is copyright © 2016 Caryl Churchill Limited

Here We Go and Escaped Alone: Two Plays is published by Theatre Communications Group, Inc., 520 Eighth Avenue, 24th Floor, New York, NY 10018-4156.

This volume is published in arrangement with Nick Hern Books Limited, The Glasshouse, 49a Goldhawk Road, London, W12 8QP.

This publication of *Here We Go and Escaped Alone: Two Plays* by Caryl Churchill, through TCG's Book Program, is made possible in part by the New York State Council on the Arts with the support of Governor Andrew Cuomo and the New York State Legislature.

TCG books are exclusively distributed to the book trade by Consortium Book Sales and Distribution.

A catalog record for this book is available from the Library of Congress.

ISBN 978-1-55936-540-6 (paperback)

Front cover image by Vangelis Paterakis

Cover design by Lisa Govan

First TCG Edition, October 2016
Second Printing, February 2020

Contents

HERE WE GO

Here We Go was first performed in the Lyttelton auditorium of the National Theatre, London, on 27 November 2015 (previews from 25 November). The cast was as follows:

Madeline Appiah
Susan Engel
Patrick Godfrey
Hazel Holder
Joshua James
Amanda Lawrence
Stuart McQuarrie
Eleanor Matsuura
Alan Williams

Director	Dominic Cooke
Designer	Vicki Mortimer
Lighting Designer	Guy Hoare
Sound Designer	Christopher Shutt
Visual Effects	Chris Fisher
Company Voice Work	Jeannette Nelson
Staff Director	Rosemary McKenna
Stage Manager	Andrew Speed
Deputy Stage Manager	Fran Redvers-Jones

The number of actors can vary in different productions. Not fewer than three in the first scene and not more than eight – five or six is probably good. Age and gender can also be decided. The character in 'After' can be but needn't be the man whose funeral it is in the first scene. Same with 'Getting There', and the carer may or may not be someone we've met before.

1. HERE WE GO

*The speeches at the end of the scene are to be inserted at random
during the dialogue. There are ten – use as many as you need for each
character to have one.*

The place is a party after a funeral.

We miss him

of course

everyone

but his closest

because friendship was

wider range of acquaintance than anyone I've ever

gift

closeness

listened

and so witty I remember him saying

listened and understood

always seemed

though of course *are* you any wiser when you're older I
feel sixteen all the time

all he'd lived through

the war the war not so many people left who

and Spain even imagine

what how old

no he did

and he never actually joined the party because of what
they did to the anarchists so

not that he was an anarchist

unless sexually

well yes there

and is the third wife here are they all

in the red hat

isn't that the daughter?

no the big red

and is that her partner with the beard?

all the women seem

yes they all kiss but I wonder

except of course

she's keeping very quiet

love of his life

they say

though he was an old goat

of course

such charm was the thing

yes because he didn't look

oh when he was young

none of us can remember

well I can

of course

he was a vision at thirty

and photos photos have you seen there are some on the table in the

yes on a horse, about twelve

but his mind

yes his mind

extraordinary mind

literature of course but also

literature of France, Spain, Russia, every South American

physics, he had an extremely scientific

could have been

never fully

an mp in the fifties

I never knew

oh yes

which party

well obviously

yes but he was a libertarian

man of the left

always fell out

a bit too much of an individualist some might

just quarrelsome

but then he'd make it up with a bunch of flowers

I always remember a time he

and did you meet his friend Bill?

who isn't here or is he?

would we recognise?

heavy drinker

he put it away himself

but could always carry

champagne in hospital

so wonderful

never complained

well he did

terrible temper

I never saw

swore at the nurses

well I suppose anyone

yes pain

pain does change

horrible to see

morphine

can make you feel very happy, when I broke my pelvis

or sick

confused

sounded as if he was demented but of course we knew
it was

though he always did have a temper

I never saw

perhaps you didn't annoy

only the people who were closest

no, people he didn't know, cold-callers

van drivers

dogs

dogs?

he hated

never knew that

cats cats cats

yes what's going to happen

his daughter said she could take the old ginger tom but

in a flat?

cats like places of course more than people, they

your cat?

stopped being sick everywhere thank god, the vet's bills

and how are you keeping now you're

yes fantastic

wonderful job

New York in the morning so I can't stay too long I've got to

promotion

still hoping

painting

out of work so long now I

keeping busy

your new partner I hear

getting married

and you always said

yes but love when it really

yes

you don't quite expect

so happy for you

yes after all those

and we're expecting a baby in September but don't

so great

just close friends till

of course

another drink

have to remember I'm driving so

see all these people

yes because we hardly ever

and so many people I've never set eyes

all his different walks of

who've known him for sixty years

only met him last summer but he

talking to one of the carers

closer to him at the end I think than

well someone who washes

and wipes

you do love who you look after and who looks after you
like that's how with babies

or cats

all one way with cats

no stroking them reduces our

lovely service

favourite

but he wasn't a Christian surely or was it his

but what do you do?

plenty of people nowadays, pop songs, poems

yes despite everything he was rather

I don't think he cared, he's not the type who'd plan

no, plan their own service, oh dear

must keep an eye on the time

far to go?

came on the M23 and the roadworks at junction

go back through

long way round

stay overnight

long day tomorrow

I did cry

no I never actually have at a funeral

what sort of

self-pity and anger mainly I'm afraid, so

but that sort of lofty

uplifting

some bits of music

but not today's for me

no but the thought

yes hard to believe he's gone even though

it comes at you suddenly doesn't it

like stepping on a rake

I know after my mother

well parents of course are a different

not really

because then you're next

but you think your friend's still there in a different city and
not seeing them is

yes and then it hits you you'll never

and I find I can't remember voices

no not for long

we should all be recorded

please no, photographs are bad enough

oh but I love

let it go and just remember whatever we

the oddest things

can see him standing on one leg, I think it was in France
were you there

no I never went to that house just to the one in what was
that street?

very funny

he was

he could tell a joke

yes I can never remember

One of these is spoken by each of the characters directly to the audience. They should be inserted randomly into the previous dialogue in any order. The number of years later can be adjusted if necessary to make sense for the characters.

I die the next day. I'm knocked over by a motorbike crossing a road in North London. I think I can get over while the light's red but I'm looking for cars. I'm dead before the ambulance comes and it comes very quickly.

I die eleven years later. I have a heart attack swimming in the North Sea in January. I'd done it before all right.

I die thirty-eight years later of lung cancer. I hadn't realised before that you have different kinds of cancer depending on where it starts so you can have breast cancer in your brain, and I have lung cancer in my liver. I don't find the pain relief as helpful as I'd hoped.

I die five years later stabbed by an intruder. I keep a knife by the bed and when I brandish it he snatches it. He's shocked by the blood, he's saying sorry sorry and then I pass out.

I die twenty-six years later. I slip over on the icy steps going to put out the rubbish and break my hip, and my chest gets worse lying in bed. I have given up smoking but a bit late.

I die forty years later in my sleep, which is a relief. I was expecting to live to see the baby.

I die seven years later of a brain tumour. It takes a while for the doctors to pay attention to the headaches but maybe it would have spread anyway.

I die sixty-two years later. More and more things aren't working. They put pneumonia on the death certificate.

I die twenty-three years later after nine years of Alzheimer's. I don't know anyone who's there.

I die six months later. I hang myself. I should have thought about who'd find me.

2. AFTER

One person. Very fast.

Falling falling down the tunnel down the tunnel a tunnel a
light a train a tube train aaah coming to kill me

but I'm already dead is that right and ah here I am
arrived somewhere and hello is that grandpa?

surely not greater light and further shore no

but is this the pearly gates yes look actual pearls and that's
St Peter beard key

but I don't believe anything like

and it's gone is anyone there hello

there must be vast numbers of us that's a comfort far
more than the living

except of course there used to be fewer living at any one
time so maybe the living now equal all the dead could that
be but even so there are billions right back to cave and
where are they

oh there they are here we are I'm just a speck of sand in a
desert oh

or what is this are we all standing on the Isle of Wight it's
worse than the tube at rush hour I can't get my face away
from his back I don't want

ah that's better they've gone I'm on my own

I'm on my own

and what's happened to me what's going to happen I
always was afraid despite everything there'd be a
judgement and I'd be a goat not a sheep thinking of
those herds in North Africa where they're mixed together
and it can be hard to tell I understood the metaphor then
very good

and I think they don't emphasise hell these days but you
can't be sure because there's nothing kind about the
universe just rushing apart

and even our little place in it we evolved to belong has
hurricanes and cancer and is kind for some but often
unkind and they have to live with foul water or wake up in
dread and what would it be like to have to live your life as
someone obsessed with having sex with children or
wanting to kill what would you do with that

and it might not be fair to punish them but it may not be
fair because the universe isn't so who says god is if there is
one here somewhere

and hell used to be mediaeval tortures pincers and fire
and we thought god can't do that because no one would
do that

but we know people do just that sort of thing quite a lot so
maybe there is a hell of arms chopped off and piles of
bodies with bags on their heads and hanging upside down
ah why shouldn't I be one of the people who deserve that

if deserving comes into it it might be random

because I'm the rich camel who can't get through
compared to oh I know there's mega how reassuring
yachts but no I was comfortable comfortable in my life
chicken and a warm bed

and how much good did I very little because I was always
loving someone or organising something or looking at
trees or having a quiet sit-down with the paper and I'm
sorry I'm sorry

or is it purgatory do they have that still where it's burned
out of you not for ever yes I can feel it getting hotter the
blast of it on my

ridiculous I don't believe it of course never did that's not
happening there's plenty of other something completely

yes here comes aah his head's what a wild dog fox jackal
that's it not a mask he's

and that one's a bird ibis long curved sharp I'm sorry I'm
sorry

and here are the scales there's a feather in one pan so I
take out my heart and put it in the other and surely it
can't be light as a feather and if it weighs the pan down I
get thrown to that lion hippo crocodile and will I pass out
as I feel its hot breath sometimes people go into a swoon
of shock when an animal has them in its mouth National
Geographic probably and then I would really be dead and
gone I suppose

which ancient religion is this anyway Egypt

surely I must be in for something more Nordic

Thor with a thunderbolt

valhalla or is that just for war heroes yes there they are
sitting round the table drunk and roaring not my idea
of fun

and for illness or old age here's a blue black giantess
come to take me somewhere bleaker maybe a cold beach
with a wind I once went swimming I'd rather a warm
Greek white stones can I have that and is that Charon in
the boat I can get in wobble sit down and over the dark
river we go

I've always been scared of guard dogs so I hope Cerberus

and do I have to gibber with those bloodless dead did
Odysseus go to see them yes I can see him coming now
and here we are all stretching out our hands to him

but he won't do anything for me living so long after his
time and surely he's fictional anyway so how can he
help me get out of this hanging about and hanging
about for ever when I could be doing something like
going back and

walk haunt turn the room cold hear them talking and long
for someone to see me here I'm here my love can't you see
me hundreds of years still floating through walls I'm here
I'm here no I'm not a ghost story

going back and having another life my own life over again
like that movie and do it better of course because most of
the time I hardly noticed it going by and I used to look
back and think how careless I was when I was young I
never noticed and by then I was middle-aged and later I'd
look back and think *then* I never noticed

and another go would be welcome

but nobody suggests they do that in real life real death not
another go as yourself another go as somebody else or of
course some*thing* else

and have I lived the sort of life that would get me one step
up to be a happier better person one true love maybe I
deserve to paint or

no not be in power hate to be a president king general
imagine how terrible that might be a punishment of
course a step down

or I might have to sleep in the street yes I'm walking
miles with a heavy sick child I'm so depressed I can't put
on my socks

but I might not be human a bird a bird everyone wants to
fly oh a kestrel can I be a kestrel yes I can see every blade
of grass and a mouse drop on the mouse but I might be
the mouse

I might be a rabid street dog foaming a cow up the ramp
to the slaughter

I'd rather be an endangered species some beautiful far far
anywhere oh

I might be an insect one of billions I am already one of
billions but trillions

a locust eating and eating do they feel joy do they just eat
or maybe a flea blood and the amazing jump

oh I don't want to be the caterpillar the wasp lays an egg
in and it hatches and consumes from inside

but surely that's not a belief I've ever I've never

and I wouldn't be me this one I've been doesn't remember
others it's extinction of me even if I'm part of some
cosmic whatsit drop gone back to the ocean no

and of course all the bits of my body are on their way
now breaking down into smaller and smaller rather
disgusting at first but into the daisies

or did they have me cremated how odd I don't know in
which case it's all gone up in smoke leaving just those
gritty ashes that might be partly someone else's I'm not
sure how particular they are at the crem when they sweep
it out

but anyway all the chemicals atoms neutrons from stars on
their way because the energy's still all there

but not my energy like 'oh I'm so tired today I've got no
energy' now I've really got no energy it's somewhere else
like before I was born

all those atoms are somewhere else

and you're just a thing that happens like an elephant or a
daffodil

and there you all are for a short time

that's how it's put together for a short time

and oddly you are actually are one of those

and it goes on and on and you're used to it and then
suddenly

3. GETTING THERE

A very old or ill person and a carer.

The old/ill person is in nightclothes and is helped by the carer to get dressed, slowly and with difficulty because of pain and restricted movement.

Then to get undressed and back into nightclothes.

Then to get dressed.

Then to get undressed and back into nightclothes.

Then to get dressed…

for as long as the scene lasts.

End.

ESCAPED ALONE

'I only am escaped alone to tell thee.'

Book of Job. Moby Dick.

Escaped Alone was first performed at the Royal Court
Jerwood Theatre Downstairs, London, on 21 January 2016.
The cast was as follows:

MRS JARRETT   Linda Bassett
SALLY   Deborah Findlay
LENA   Kika Markham
VI   June Watson

Director	James Macdonald
Designer	Miriam Buether
Lighting Designer	Peter Mumford
Sound Designer	Christopher Shutt
Casting Director	Amy Ball
Assistant Director	Roy Alexander Weise
Production Manager	Tariq Rifaat
Costume Supervisor	Lucy Walshaw
Stage Manager	Kate McDowell
Assistant Stage Manager	Rachel Hendry

Characters

SALLY
VI
LENA
MRS JARRETT

They are all at least seventy.

Place

Sally's backyard.

Several unmatching chairs. Maybe one's a kitchen chair.

Time

Summer afternoon.

A number of afternoons but the action is continuous.

1.

MRS J	I'm walking down the street and there's a door in the fence open and inside are three women I've seen before.
VI	Don't look now but there's someone watching us.
LENA	Is it that woman?
SALLY	Is that you, Mrs Jarrett?
MRS J	So I go in.

SALLY	Rosie locked out in the rain
VI	forgot her key
SALLY	climbed over
LENA	lucky to have neighbours who
SALLY	such a high wall
VI	this is Rosie her granddaughter
MRS J	I've a son, Frank
VI	I've a son
MRS J	suffers from insomnia
VI	doesn't come very often. But Thomas
LENA	that's her nephew
SALLY	he'd knock up the shelves in no time
VI	a big table
SALLY	grain of the wood
VI	a table like that would last a lifetime

SALLY	an heirloom
LENA	except we all eat off our laps
MRS J	nothing like a table
LENA	I like a table
VI	all have each other's keys because there's no way round and anyway I couldn't climb
MRS J	unless you lose them
VI	no I hang them all on a nail
SALLY	in a teapot
VI	teapot?
SALLY	Elsie puts them in and takes them out
LENA	down the floorboards
VI	only use bags in mugs
SALLY	holds your finger and then takes one step and down she goes.
LENA	Barney never out of his phone
VI	I'd have been the same
LENA	looking pale
VI	whole worlds in your pocket
LENA	little bit worried about Kevin and Mary, never hear an endearment
SALLY	but nobody ever knows
MRS J	you'd be surprised what goes on
LENA	twenty years in June
VI	we had to wear hats
SALLY	a pink one and I didn't
VI	so you gave it to Angela

SALLY   I'd forgotten Angela

LENA   shadows under her eyes

VI   ended up with a green one and it didn't suit you

LENA   I could never say a word of course.

VI   And Maisie, never so happy

LENA   that's her niece

SALLY   quantum

VI   I can't really follow

SALLY   I can't even add up

LENA   they don't add up any more

VI   particles and waves I can manage but after that

SALLY   always good at sums as a child, she'd say two big
          numbers

VI   and while we were carrying things in our head

LENA   I needed a pencil

SALLY   she'd say the answer and it was always right

MRS J   I could always make change quick with the
          shillings and pence

VI   we'd be the ones got it wrong

LENA   easier now it's decimal

SALLY   always right.

LENA   And Vera

MRS J   Four hundred thousand tons of rock paid for by
         senior executives split off the hillside to smash
         through the roofs, each fragment onto the
         designated child's head. Villages were buried and
         new communities of survivors underground
         developed skills of feeding off the dead where
         possible and communicating with taps and groans.
         Instant celebrities rose on ropes to the light of
         flashes. Time passed. Rats were eaten by those
         who still had digestive systems, and mushrooms
         were traded for urine. Babies were born and
         quickly became blind. Some groups lost their
         sexuality while others developed a new morality of
         constant fucking with any proximate body. A
         young woman crawling from one society to the
         other became wedged, only her head reaching her
         new companions. Stories of those above ground
         were told and retold till there were myths of the
         husband who cooked feasts, the wife who swam
         the ocean, the gay lover who could fly, the child
         who read minds, the talking dog. Prayers were said
         to them and various sects developed with tolerance
         and bitter hatred. Songs were sung until dry
         throats caused the end of speech. Torrential rain
         leaked through cracks and flooded the tunnels
         enabling screams at last before drownings.
         Survivors were now solitary and went insane at
         different rates.

2.

SALLY	corner shop
LENA	don't like the
VI	mini Tesco
LENA	bit far
MRS J	used to be the fish and chip shop
VI	that other one's gone
SALLY	the old grocer
VI	I'd do a shop for seventeen shillings
LENA	so what's that in
MRS J	fifteen's seventy-five p
VI	but we earned nothing too
SALLY	so who does the shopping if you can't go out?
LENA	I do go
VI	is Kevin a help?
SALLY	I could always
VI	but it's good for you to go yourself
SALLY	good to get out
LENA	I do get out
SALLY	you're here
LENA	it's not easy
SALLY	antique shop now but in between it was that café
VI	it was never a café

SALLY	the Blue something, an animal
MRS J	I been there
SALLY	Hedgehog, something unlikely
VI	I don't think so
SALLY	maybe it was when
LENA	oh
SALLY	that would be it of course
VI	I did miss a few things when I was away
MRS J	away was you?
LENA	just a little while
VI	six years
SALLY	that's what it was then, Blue Antelope
VI	antique shops now but down the other end
SALLY	yes three shops boarded up
VI	that's the nail parlour and the old dentist
SALLY	did you ever go?
VI	he was terrible
SALLY	he was such a bad
VI	'this might just trouble you a little'
SALLY	oh my god
VI	half an hour to get there but so much better
LENA	I should go to the dentist
SALLY	a checkup
LENA	it must be five years
MRS J	you don't want toothache
LENA	it's just one more thing you have to do, one thing after another, I can't seem to

SALLY	I could always go with you
LENA	if I go
SALLY	or do some shopping
VI	it's good she gets out herself
LENA	I do get out
SALLY	and the chicken nuggets closed down
VI	that was the ironmongers
SALLY	no in between it was the health shop
LENA	a hammer and a spade
VI	there must be quite a few things I missed
SALLY	not really, it all goes by, I can't remember those years specially
VI	remember what was happening where I was of course
SALLY	yes of course
VI	though it gets to be a blur because it's all a bit the same
SALLY	it must have been
VI	unless there was an excitement like a fight
MRS J	fights was there?
VI	or love affairs
LENA	I do get out it's just difficult

MRS J   First the baths overflowed as water was
        deliberately wasted in a campaign to punish the
        thirsty. Swimming pools engulfed the leisure
        centres and coffee ran down the table legs. Rivers
        flowed back towards their tributaries and up the
        streams to what had been trickles in moss. Ponies
        climbed to high ground and huddled with the
        tourists. Yawls, ketches, kayaks, canoes, schooners,
        planks, dinghies, lifebelts and upturned umbrellas,
        swimming instructors and lilos, rubber ducks and
        pumice stone floated on the stock market. Waves
        engulfed ferris wheels and drowned bodies were
        piled up to block doors. Then the walls of water
        came from the sea. Villages vanished and cities
        relocated to their rooftops. Sometimes children fell
        down the sewage chutes but others caught seagulls
        with kites. Some died of thirst, some of drinking
        the water. When the flood receded thousands
        stayed on the roofs fed by helicopter while heroes
        and bonded workers shovelled the muck into
        buckets that were stored in the flood museums.

3.

VI	Parallel universes
SALLY	fiction
VI	scientists
SALLY	makes good stories
VI	second series
LENA	I'm watching the third
SALLY	does Elliott
MRS J	don't tell us
SALLY	too many universes for me
LENA	when I stay home I watch
VI	you've seen everything
SALLY	but you're feeling better
LENA	it just drops away, you wake up one morning and it's all right
SALLY	amazing
LENA	like a different world
VI	universe
MRS J	I don't like Elliott
VI	the way he looks at his wife
LENA	but you're meant to think that
SALLY	I do think that, I don't care
VI	and now the money

SALLY   Ursula's nasty

VI   I'm sorry for Ursula

SALLY   I think it's going to be Ursula

MRS J   four husbands

LENA   they want you to think that

VI   loved her in the first series

LENA   exactly

SALLY   but universes to get your mind round

LENA   the third series

VI   and the very very small

SALLY   yes our bodies

VI   millions of little creatures

LENA   makes my flesh creep

VI   fleas on a cat

LENA   microbes on a flea

VI   oh

LENA   oh

VI   sorry

LENA   look what you've done

MRS J   what's she done?

LENA   we don't mention

VI   are you all right?

MRS J   what, fleas?

VI   no

LENA   cats

VI   shh

LENA	are you all right?
SALLY	yes I'm fine thank you
VI	sorry I'm so sorry
SALLY	the third series
LENA	particles
VI	though mind you are we helping by never saying?
LENA	don't start that
SALLY	it's all right, you needn't
VI	shouldn't we just say it, say black and white, tabby, longhaired, shorthaired, siamese
MRS J	I've got a lovely tabby but he's a tom so
LENA	stop it
VI	expose her to it and nothing bad happens and she gets used to nothing bad
LENA	stop it
VI	I'm helping
MRS J	is she going to faint?
SALLY	no no I'm
LENA	see?
VI	I'm sorry I just get
SALLY	I know it's stupid
VI	no
SALLY	I know you hate me sometimes
VI	no, I
LENA	see?
SALLY	you just need to face
VI	I need to face?
SALLY	how unpleasant you can be

LENA   see?

VI   oh it's me now, it's always someone

LENA   stop it

MRS J   let's hear it

SALLY   it doesn't bother me

VI   oh let's not

SALLY   it's fine

VI   I know I shouldn't

SALLY   so tell us about the third series

MRS J   don't tell us about the third series

LENA   I'll just hint that Elliott

VI   don't say it

MRS J   The chemicals leaked through cracks in the money.
The first symptoms were irritability and nausea.
Domestic violence increased and there were
incidents on the underground. School absenteeism
tripled and ninety-seven schools were taken into
special measures. Dog owners cleared up their pets'
vomit or risked a fine. Miscarriages were frequent
leading to an increase of opportunities in grief
counselling. Birth deformities outpaced the
immigration of plastic surgeons. Gas masks were
available on the NHS with a three-month waiting
time and privately in a range of colours.
Sometimes the cancers began in the lungs and
sometimes on the fingertips or laptops. The
remaining citizens were evacuated to camps in
northern Canada where they were sprayed and
victimised, and the city was left to sick foxes, who
soon abandoned it for lack of dustbins.

4.

LENA	So how many noughts
VI	a billion has nine
SALLY	no
VI	a trillion
SALLY	a billion has twelve
VI	no, we adopted the American
SALLY	are you saying a billion isn't a million million?
VI	a thousand million now, and a trillion
SALLY	oh I don't like that
MRS J	what's a zillion?
VI	and then of course you get a googol and a googolplex, which isn't the same as
LENA	a zillion's what you say, is it a real
VI	three Brazilians dead and President Bush said Oh no, remind me how many is a brazilian
SALLY	he's taken the place of moron
LENA	moron?
SALLY	when I was a child Little Moron jokes for anything stupid, what did the Little Moron say when he
VI	what did he say?
LENA	no one says moron
SALLY	they keep having to change what you can say because whatever word they use becomes

VI	did we ever say moron for jokes? is it American or
LENA	but you can't even make that kind of joke not about mentally
SALLY	Irish for a long time, Irish jokes
MRS J	'no blacks no dogs no Irish'
SALLY	I remember that
VI	and we weren't even that shocked
LENA	we do shock easier
VI	but you have to have jokes about stupid things someone might do because anyone might, it's funny
LENA	you can't have a class of people
SALLY	you could have yourself
VI	you could have me
SALLY	what did I say when I jumped off the top of
VI	don't the comedians do that, they make themselves
SALLY	but of course we know they're clever.
LENA	So in other countries do they have that?
VI	jokes about being stupid?
LENA	making out it's some neighbour who's
SALLY	you always get people hating their neighbours
VI	yes the closer they are
SALLY	Serbs and Croats, French and English
LENA	there's history though
SALLY	but anyone everyone outside thinks is the same
VI	Catholics and Protestants, Sunni and Shia
MRS J	Arsenal and Tottenham

SALLY	there you are
LENA	Cain and Abel
VI	did Abel make jokes about Cain being stupid and that's why he killed him?
LENA	odd they needed a story about how killing started because
SALLY	chimpanzees
LENA	but you do wonder why of course so you make a story
VI	easily done I found
SALLY	different each time
VI	I don't know why, I never knew why
MRS J	found it easy did you?
LENA	never mind that
SALLY	not always easy and a lot of men in the war never fired their guns because
VI	no it's all right, she can know
MRS J	what can I know?
VI	tell her, go on
LENA	she accidentally
SALLY	a long time ago
LENA	accidentally killed her husband
VI	not accidentally
LENA	in self defence
MRS J	how did you do that?
VI	kitchen knife happened to be in my hand
LENA	just bad luck really

VI   so when I hit back

MRS J   so that was all right was it, self defence

SALLY   more complicated

LENA   the lawyers

SALLY   manslaughter

VI   six years, which was half

MRS J   still a long time

VI   the first two years

LENA   things do speed up

SALLY   everything does

MRS J   you get used to it

SALLY   so that can be good but when it's your whole life
            speeding up

LENA   don't start on that

SALLY   I'd like to have time travel

VI   knock knock

LENA   who's there?

VI   Dr

SALLY   that's a six-year-old's joke.

MRS J   The hunger began when eighty per cent of food was diverted to tv programmes. Commuters watched breakfast on iPlayer on their way to work. Smartphones were distributed by charities when rice ran out, so the dying could watch cooking. The entire food stock of Newcastle was won by lottery ticket and the winner taken to a 24 hour dining room where fifty chefs chopped in relays and the public voted on what he should eat next. Cars were traded for used meat. Children fell asleep in class and didn't wake up. The obese sold slices of themselves until hunger drove them to eat their own rashers. Finally the starving stormed the tv centres and were slaughtered and smoked in large numbers. Only when cooking shows were overtaken by sex with football teams did cream trickle back to the shops and rice was airlifted again.

5.

VI	People always want to fly
LENA	fly like a bird
SALLY	that's always the favourite, what would you like
LENA	invisible
VI	languages, I'd like to be able to speak every
SALLY	but we do fly now
MRS J	planes isn't the same
VI	go to any country at all and understand
SALLY	and nobody looks out of the window
LENA	watching the screens
VI	I do like getting all those movies I never
SALLY	looking down on clouds
LENA	yes what would Julius Caesar have thought or
SALLY	and they make it like being in a very unpleasant room
VI	try to make you forget you're up in the air
LENA	because it could be frightening being up in the air
SALLY	because that's not what people mean by flying
VI	flying like a bird in the sky
LENA	but if people could, if we all
VI	that's no good
LENA	imagine the crowds
SALLY	at rush hour

LENA	separate lanes
SALLY	flocks
VI	like starlings, that would be good, all those shapes
LENA	flocks of pigeons, they seem to change colour
SALLY	no we wouldn't have that sense of each other, we'd keep bumping
VI	but what people want is fly by yourself
LENA	straight up like a lark
VI	or hover like what?
LENA	a kestrel
VI	kestrel yes
LENA	or an eagle
VI	soar like an eagle
MRS J	I wouldn't want to be a pigeon
VI	we're not being birds we're us but able to
SALLY	pigeons are like rats
LENA	pigeons are not
VI	looking down from above
SALLY	like drones with cameras
LENA	Barney's got one, remote control, you can see as if you're
VI	I hate that because they bomb and they're not in danger
LENA	it's just a toy
SALLY	is it all right to bomb if you are in danger?
VI	but no it's not the seeing it's the sensation
LENA	soaring and diving

SALLY   like swimming under water really going up and
            down

VI   no only if you can scuba

LENA   hate putting my head under water

VI   birds is better than fish

MRS J   I wouldn't want to be a fish

LENA   or being invisible is the one I'd like

SALLY   all this about birds, I don't quite like about birds
            because birds leads to cats, pigeons leads to cats, cat
            among the pigeons, next door's tabby had a pigeon
            such flapping and couldn't kill it, wouldn't, just
            played about kept grabbing it again and the bird
            was maimed someone had to ugh, and pigeons like
            rats leads to cats rats cats rats are filthy plague
            everywhere, only how many feet from a rat, and
            pigeons are filthy, rats are filthy, cats are filthy their
            bites are poison they bite you and the bite festers,
            but that's not it that's not it I know that's just an
            excuse to give a reason I know I've no reason I
            know it's just cats cats themselves are the horror
            because they're cats and I have to keep them out I
            have to make sure I never think about a cat because
            if I do I have to make sure there's no cats and they
            could be anywhere they could get in a window I
            have to go round the house and make sure all the
            windows are locked and I don't know if I checked
            properly I can't remember I was too frightened to
            notice I have to go round the windows again I have
            to go round the windows again back to the kitchen
            back to the bedroom back to the kitchen back to the
            bedroom the bathroom back to the kitchen back to
            the door, the door might blow open if it's windy
            even if it's not windy suppose the postman was
            putting a large packet and pushed the door and it
            came open because it wasn't properly shut and then
            a cat because they can get through very very small

and once they're in they could be anywhere they could be under the bed in the wardrobe up on the top shelf with the winter sweaters that would be a place for a cat to sleep or in a wastepaper basket or under the cushions on the sofa or in the cupboard with the saucepans or in the cupboard with the food a cat could curl up on the cans of tomatoes a cat could be in with the jam and honey a cat could be in the biscuit tin, a cat could be in the fridge in the freezer in the salad drawer in the box of cheese in the broom cupboard the mop bucket a cat could be in the oven the top oven under the lid of the casserole in a box of matches behind a picture under a rug back to the bedroom a cat could be under the bed in the duvet in the pillowcase in the wardrobe a cat could be in a shoe on a hanger under my dress in a woolly hat inside a coat sleeve a cat could be in any of the drawers so I tip them all out and shake every – cat behind the books on the shelf behind the dvds a cat could be in the teapot with the keys a cat could be on the ceiling a cat could be on top of the door a cat could be behind me a cat could be under my hand when I put out my hand. I need someone to say there's no cats, I need to say to someone do you smell cat, I need to say do you think there's any way a cat could have got in, and they have to say of course not, they have to say of course not, I have to believe them, it has to be someone I believe, I have to believe they're not just saying it, I have to believe they know there are no cats, I have to believe there are no cats. And then briefly the joy of that.

LENA	Eagles you get eagles as national
VI	eagles are fascist
LENA	America has the eagle
VI	well

MRS J   I wouldn't mind being an eagle

SALLY   very often fascist

LENA   shame for the eagle really, it little knows

VI   an eagle wouldn't have much empathy

SALLY   nor would a blackbird come to that

VI   you don't get blackbirds as national

LENA   do religions have birds?

VI   dove of peace

SALLY   sacred ibis

LENA   you could have bird rituals

SALLY   scattering of birdseed

VI   bird calls by the congregation

LENA   holy ghost of course that gets pictured sometimes as

SALLY   that's the dove of peace

VI   I thought the holy ghost was invisible

LENA   I'd rather be invisible myself.

MRS J   The wind developed by property developers
          started as breezes on cheeks and soon turned
          heads inside out. The army fired nets to catch
          flying cars but most spun by with dozens clinging
          and shrieking, dropping off slowly. Buildings
          migrated from London to Lahore, Kyoto to
          Kansas City, and survivors were interned for
          having no travel documents. Some in the
          whirlwind went higher and higher, the airsick
          families taking selfies in case they could ever share
          them. Shanty towns were cleared. Pets rained from
          the sky. A kitten became famous.

6.

All sing. **SALLY**, **VI** *and* **LENA** *in harmony.* **MRS JARRETT** *joins in the melody. They are singing for themselves in the garden, not performing to the audience.*

MRS J The illness started when children drank sugar developed from monkeys. Hair fell out, feet swelled, organs atrophied. Hairs blowing in the wind rapidly passed round the world. When they fell into the ocean cod died and fishermen blew up each other's boats. Planes with sick passengers were diverted to Antarctica. Some got into bed with their dead, others locked the doors and ran till they fell down. Volunteers and conscripts over seven nursed the sick and collected bodies. Governments cleansed infected areas and made deals with allies to bomb each other's capitals. Presidents committed suicide. The last survivors had immunity and the virus mutated, exterminating plankton.

7.

SALLY	I miss work
VI	I don't miss work at all
SALLY	you're learning Spanish
VI	you're in love
SALLY	a little
MRS J	in love are you?
VI	your job was far
SALLY	could be very boring of course
VI	no all the people and all
SALLY	yes but endless colds coughs coughs sore throats coughs
VI	'antibiotics please'
SALLY	and of course you have to be alert
VI	because sometimes
SALLY	you don't want to miss cancer
VI	did you ever?
SALLY	terrible occasion
MRS J	I go to that Dr Meadows
SALLY	reliable though
MRS J	but you can't get an appointment
VI	envy you doing good
SALLY	made your clients happy

MRS J	what did you
VI	hairdresser
MRS J	cut my own hair, cut my husband's hair
SALLY	tell you their troubles
VI	they did
MRS J	didn't look very good mind
SALLY	and you didn't have to fix the troubles just fix the hair
VI	that's true
SALLY	while I was supposed to fix
VI	and you could sometimes
SALLY	sometimes I could
VI	because hair's a bit trivial
SALLY	yes but you can feel quite new with a different
VI	or miserable if you don't like it
SALLY	the first day or two
VI	kept coming back every couple of days
SALLY	shorter and shorter?
VI	shorter, different colours, I finally had to
MRS J	the hair wasn't the problem
VI	it wasn't the problem
SALLY	and you really don't miss it
VI	I do now we're talking about
SALLY	though I do enjoy the days
VI	yes having the afternoons
MRS J	when I was a lollipop lady a few years back

SALLY   that's afternoon work of course and morning and
            lunchtime

MRS J   give it up after a month

LENA   I couldn't keep on

VI   you loved that office

LENA   I did

VI   such a highflying

LENA   some days it would be all right for weeks but then
            I'd find it coming down again. You're so far away
            from people at the next desk. Email was better than
            speaking. It's down now.
            Why can't I just?
            I just can't.
            I sat on the bed this morning and didn't stand up
            till lunchtime. The air was too thick. It's hard to
            move, it's hard to see why you'd move.
            It's not so bad in the afternoon, I got myself here.
            I don't like it here. I've no interest.
            Why talk about that? Why move your mouth and
            do talking? Why see anyone? Why know about
            anyone?
            It was half past three and all this time later it's
            twenty-five to four.
            If I think about a place I could be where there's
            something nice like the sea that would be worse
            because the sea would be the same as an empty
            room so it's better to be in the empty room
            because then there's fewer things to mean nothing
            at all.
            I'd rather hear something bad than something
            good. I'd rather hear nothing.
            It's still just the same.
            It's just the same.
            It's the same.

SALLY   Your medication doesn't seem very

VI   do you take it?

LENA   it's not an easy thing to

SALLY   not a sprained ankle

MRS J   I had my hips done

VI   and is that

MRS J   two new hips I can walk all day

SALLY   my knee

VI   my back doing hair on my feet all day

SALLY   yes at least I sat

VI   exactly

SALLY   but then I ran

VI   I missed it when I had to stop

MRS J   was that when you was

VI   four years

MRS J   did you go back to hair after?

VI   not the same place, it was never such a good

SALLY   you did several different

VI   out of work completely a long time

MRS J   not fair because it was just self defence was it

VI   it was

LENA   not fair really

SALLY   more complicated

LENA   self defence

SALLY   fair enough really

LENA   you think?

SALLY   because if I'd said

LENA	said what?
SALLY	said what happened
LENA	what happened?
SALLY	it was complicated
MRS J	you was there was you?
SALLY	in the kitchen
VI	you'd had a drink of course
SALLY	we all had, that's why
VI	are you saying
SALLY	I'm just saying I didn't quite
VI	what? come on what? are you saying
SALLY	I didn't tell it quite how it was because
VI	you did
SALLY	no because I took into account what he was like
LENA	it wasn't murder
SALLY	could have been that's all I'm saying if I hadn't
VI	if you hadn't what?
SALLY	hadn't said it in a way that worked out
MRS J	lied in the witness box did you?
SALLY	she's my friend, of course I
VI	you thought you were lying
SALLY	I thought I was economical
VI	you think I murdered him?
SALLY	it's not a matter really of defining
VI	you think I'm a murderer?

SALLY   it doesn't really

VI   all this time you've thought

SALLY   it was so long ago

VI   you think

SALLY   I don't care if you are

VI   I care

SALLY   so long ago

VI   you think

SALLY   look I'm sorry

VI   no what

SALLY   sorry, I shouldn't have

VI   what

SALLY   I don't know what I mean even

LENA   what did you say?

SALLY   I don't even know what I said any more

MRS J   what did you see?

SALLY   certainly don't know what I saw any more

VI   you think I'm a murderer

SALLY   maybe you were I don't know do you think you're
          a murderer

VI   no

SALLY   okay so maybe you weren't

VI   I don't remember either

MRS J   you don't remember what you

VI   no it's gone

SALLY   there you are then.

VI   I missed cutting hair and I missed food

LENA   prison food

VI   not that I'm much of a cook

MRS J   Frank can cook

VI   I missed snacks in prison and I missed apples

MRS J   Fire broke out in ten places at once. Four cases of
          arson by children and politicians, three of
          spontaneous combustion of the markets, two of
          sunshine, one supposed by believers to be a
          punishment by God for gender dysphoria. It swept
          through saplings, petrol stations, prisons, dryads
          and books. Fires were lit to stop the fires and
          consumed squirrels, firefighters and shoppers.
          Cars sped from one furnace to another. Houses
          exploded. Some shot flaming swans, some shot
          their children. Finally the wind drove the fire to
          the ocean, where salt water made survivors faint.
          The blackened area was declared a separate
          country with zero population, zero growth and
          zero politics. Charred stumps were salvaged for art
          and biscuits.

8.

VI	Thomas finished the table
SALLY	love to see it
VI	sit round it before it goes
LENA	bought by some rich
VI	not rich rich not as if it was art
SALLY	art's ridiculous
VI	they buy it just so they can sell it they don't even look
SALLY	Rosie paints very
VI	just for yourself
LENA	and photographs I've always liked
SALLY	easy with phones
LENA	pictures of seabirds, gannets
MRS J	what's gannets?
VI	black, hold their wings out
LENA	that's cormorants
VI	puffins are the ones with beaks, I've never seen
SALLY	you'd have to go somewhere with rocks
LENA	gannets are big and white
MRS J	like a gull
LENA	bigger

SALLY   not like an albatross

VI   albatross round your neck

LENA   fly for years and years and never land.

VI   Birds can be frightening

SALLY   birds?

VI   if they swoop down

MRS J   no that's bats, they get in your hair

SALLY   they don't really

LENA   I was told as a child

SALLY   bats are worse because they zigzag

VI   'bat bat come under my hat, I'll give you a slice of
             bacon'

LENA   what's that?

VI   I don't know, I just know it

LENA   you'd hardly want it under your hat if you don't
             even like birds.

SALLY   Elsie chases birds

LENA   Elsie the dog?

VI   Elsie the dog's been dead five years

SALLY   Elsie the baby.

LENA   Dinner with Kevin and Mary

SALLY   did you get an impression

LENA   very cheerful, delicious lamb

SALLY   enjoy cooking sometimes

MRS J   Frank likes a lamb chop

LENA   I do love a kitchen

SALLY   my grandmother's kitchen

LENA   mine's more of a cupboard

SALLY   mine needs a coat of paint

LENA   would Rosie do it?

SALLY   do it myself, just need to make time

MRS J   I can't go up a ladder

LENA   that same dark orange or maybe

VI   I can't love a kitchen, I can't love a kitchen any
          more, if you've killed someone in a kitchen you're
          not going to love that kitchen, I lost that flat, even
          the kitchen where I am now reminds me of that
          kitchen, completely different colour, the cooker's on
          the other wall, and the window, but maybe it's the
          smell of food cooking, it's meat does it, cooking
          meat, the blood if it's rare, we don't often have
          meat, when you've cut somebody and seen the
          blood you don't feel the same, when he fell down
          you think oh good oh good and then you think
          that's a mistake, take that back, the horror happens
          then, keep that out, the horror is the whole thing is
          never the same, he's never a person alive
          somewhere any more, never the same with my son
          is the worst thing never forgive me how do you talk
          to a twelve-year-old when you've killed his father
          you can't explain everything the whole marriage
          what it's been like you don't want to make him hate
          his father you do want to make him hate his father
          but it wouldn't be right you don't want him to think
          you're someone who would try to make him hate
          his father, he was twelve, he'd visit me, it's hard to
          talk to a teenager if you're not seeing him all the
          time you need to be saying things like tidy your
          room have you done your homework do you want
          to watch a movie, I thought he'd be completely
          grown up but I got time off you have to do good

behaviour, six years he was eighteen he was grown up he was living by himself he'd moved up north he's got a life I'm glad he's got a life, he's got a new partner again he phones sometimes, at least he phones, that's the worst thing even worse than the blood and the thrashing about and what went wrong that's a horror but the horror goes on not seeing him he's got a life, it comes over me sometimes in the kitchen or in the night if I wake up sometimes if it's hot that's worse I can't breathe properly it all comes back in the night, but you get up in the morning and that's better put the kettle on but it's always there not there in the kitchen it's always there.

LENA	Maisie's a good cook
VI	I'm lucky with Maisie
SALLY	all those nieces
VI	I'm lucky with all those
LENA	Maisie bakes
VI	yes but not crazy baking
LENA	a nice sponge
VI	she'd do a birthday cake for her sisters.
SALLY	Rosie's going to China
VI	Rosie?
LENA	holiday or?
SALLY	university
VI	will she learn Mandarin?
LENA	always wanted to go to Japan
SALLY	get to Tesco first
VI	that's nasty
SALLY	no

VI   yes

SALLY   joke

VI   ha

LENA   I thought it was funny.

MRS J   Terrible rage terrible rage terrible rage terrible
            rage terrible rage terrible rage terrible rage terrible
            rage terrible rage terrible rage terrible rage terrible
            rage terrible rage terrible rage terrible rage terrible
            rage terrible rage terrible rage terrible rage terrible
            rage terrible rage terrible rage terrible rage terrible
            rage terrible rage

VI   Why did the chicken not cross the road?

SALLY   why did the chicken not cross the road?

VI   a car was coming

SALLY   that's just silly.

LENA   The sun's gone

VI   this time of day

SALLY   this time of year the shadow comes up earlier

LENA   still it's nice

VI   always nice to be here

MRS J   I like it here

SALLY   afternoons like this.

MRS J   And then I said thanks for the tea and I went
            home.

            End.

CARYL CHURCHILL

Caryl Churchill has written for the stage, television and radio. Her stage plays include *Owners* (Royal Court Theatre Upstairs, 1972); *Objections to Sex and Violence* (Royal Court, 1975); *Light Shining in Buckinghamshire* (Joint Stock on tour incl. Royal Court Upstairs, 1976, revived at National Theatre, 2015); *Vinegar Tom* (Monstrous Regiment on tour, incl. Half Moon and ICA, 1976); *Traps* (Royal Court Upstairs, 1977); *Cloud Nine* (Joint Stock on tour incl. Royal Court, 1979, then Theatre de Lys, New York, 1981); *Three More Sleepless Nights* (Soho Poly and Royal Court Upstairs, 1980); *Top Girls* (Royal Court, then Public Theater, New York, 1982); *Fen* (Joint Stock on tour, incl. Almeida and Royal Court, then Public Theater, New York, 1983); *Softcops* (RSC at the Pit, 1984); *A Mouthful of Birds* with David Lan (Joint Stock on tour, incl. Royal Court, 1986); *Serious Money* (Royal Court and Wyndham's, London, then Public Theater, New York, 1987); *Icecream* (Royal Court, 1989); *Mad Forest* (Central School of Speech and Drama, then Royal Court, 1990); *Lives of the Great Poisoners* with Orlando Gough and Ian Spink (Second Stride on tour, incl. Riverside Studios, London, 1991); *The Skriker* (Royal National Theatre, 1994, revived at Royal Exchange, Manchester, 2015); *Thyestes* translated from Seneca (Royal Court Upstairs, 1994); *Hotel* with Orlando Gough and Ian Spink (Second Stride on tour, incl. The Place, London, 1997); *This is a Chair* (London International Festival of Theatre at the Royal Court, 1997); *Blue Heart* (Joint Stock on tour, incl. Royal Court, 1997); *Far Away* (Royal Court Upstairs, 2000, and Albery, London, 2001, then New York Theatre Workshop, 2002); *A Number* (Royal Court Downstairs, 2002, then New York Theatre Workshop, 2004, revived at Nuffield, Southampton, 2014, then Young Vic, London, 2015); *A Dream Play* after Strindberg (Royal National Theatre, 2005); *Drunk Enough to Say I Love You?* (Royal Court Downstairs, 2006, then Public Theater, New York, 2008); *Bliss* translated from Olivier Choinière (Royal Court Upstairs, 2008); *Seven Jewish Children – a play for Gaza* (Royal Court, 2009); *Love and Information* (Royal Court Theatre Downstairs, 2012); *Ding Dong the Wicked* (Royal Court Theatre Downstairs, 2012).